from legalese to español

Legal Spanish for Busy Professionals

louis sanchez

ridiculously simple books

contents

Introduction   vii

1. ESSENTIAL SPANISH GRAMMAR   1
   Basic sentence structure   1
   Noun-adjective agreement   3
   Conjugating verbs   4
   Verb tenses   6
   Pronouns and prepositions   8
   Direct and indirect object pronouns   9
   Reflexive verbs   11
   Commands   12

2. ESSENTIAL LEGAL VOCABULARY   15
   Legal terminology   15
   Everyday vocabulary for client
   communication   17

3. BUILDING FLUENCY THROUGH
   DIALOGUES   19
   Initial client consultations   19
   Case updates and strategy discussions   21
   Negotiations and settlements   23
   Court appearances and testimonies   25

4. PRACTICE SCENARIOS AND
   ROLEPLAYS   27
   Criminal law   27
   Civil law   28
   Family law   30
   Immigration law   31

5. SPANISH LANGUAGE RESOURCES 35

Recommended Spanish-English legal dictionaries 35

Online language-learning platforms 37

Legal document translation services 39

Language exchange and practice groups 40

6. CULTURAL INSIGHTS AND TIPS 43

Understanding Hispanic culture and customs 43

Addressing clients with respect and formality 45

Avoiding language pitfalls and misunderstandings 47

7. BUILDING CONFIDENCE IN LEGAL SPANISH 51

Strategies for vocabulary retention and recall 51

Improving listening comprehension 53

Enhancing speaking proficiency 55

Embracing a growth mindset 57

8. LEGAL WRITING AND DOCUMENT REVIEW IN SPANISH 61

Tips for effective legal writing in Spanish 61

Reviewing and understanding Spanish legal documents 63

Drafting bilingual legal documents 66

9. ADVANCED LEGAL SPANISH TOPICS 69

Latin American legal systems and their distinctions 69

Navigating cultural nuances in international legal settings 71

10. CONTINUING EDUCATION AND
PROFESSIONAL DEVELOPMENT   75

Spanish-language legal conferences and
seminars   75

Study abroad and language immersion
programs   77

Networking with Spanish-speaking
legal professionals   78

Opportunities for pro bono work in
Spanish-speaking communities   80

Conclusion   83

Appendices   89

introduction

why learn spanish for legal professionals

Ah, Spanish! The melodious language of Cervantes, Shakira, and telenovelas. You might be wondering, "Why should I, a hardworking legal professional, take the time to learn Spanish?" Well, my friend, let me share some compelling reasons to set sail on this linguistic adventure – without talking like a pirate, of course.

First and foremost, let's talk numbers. With over 460 million native speakers, Spanish ranks as the second most spoken language in the world. You can find Spanish speakers in nearly every corner of the globe, from the bustling streets of Madrid to the sandy shores of the Caribbean. And, yes, even in your local courthouse.

Now, imagine for a moment that you're fluent in Spanish. As a legal professional, this newfound skill unlocks a world of opportunities. You can connect with a broader range of clients, expanding your practice and making a positive impact on countless lives. Imagine the satisfaction of bridging the language gap and providing legal counsel to someone who would have otherwise struggled to navigate the system.

And let's be honest, being bilingual is downright impressive. Picture yourself at a networking event or a dinner party, effortlessly switching between English and Spanish. Your peers will gaze at you with admiration and envy, wishing they too had taken the plunge into the world of legal Spanish.

But wait, there's more! Learning Spanish also opens the door to a rich and diverse world of culture. By mastering the language, you gain access to an incredible array of literature, film, music, and art that would have remained a mystery. And who knows, perhaps one day you'll find yourself representing a famous Spanish-speaking artist or author – wouldn't that be quite the plot twist?

Last but certainly not least, learning Spanish is good for your brain. Studies have shown that becoming bilingual can improve cognitive function, boost memory, and even delay the onset of age-related cognitive decline. So, not only will you be a more versatile legal professional, but you'll also be giving your brain a workout. It's a win-win situation.

In conclusion, why should you, a dedicated legal professional, learn Spanish? The answer is simple: it's an investment in yourself and your career. By mastering this beautiful language, you'll broaden your horizons, enhance your practice, and enrich your life in countless ways. So, let's embark on this exciting journey together, and who knows – maybe you'll even develop a taste for paella and flamenco along the way.

the importance of cultural understanding

Picture this: You've just aced your first Spanish conversation with a client. You're feeling on top of the world, ready to celebrate with a round of high-fives or maybe even a victory dance. But wait! Before you bust out your best moves, let's pause for a moment and talk about something equally important as learning the language: understanding the culture.

You see, language and culture are like two peas in a pod – or, in this case, like chips and salsa. You simply can't have one without the other. By gaining insight into the rich tapestry of Spanish-speaking cultures, you'll not only deepen your connection with your clients but also avoid potential misunderstandings that could lead to... well, let's just say some awkward moments.

For example, did you know that in many Spanish-speaking countries, punctuality isn't as strictly observed as it is in the United States? If your client shows up 15 minutes late to a meeting, don't take it personally – it's not that they don't respect your time, but rather a cultural difference in the perception of time.

Or how about personal space? In many Latin American countries, people tend to stand closer to each other during conversations. So, if a client gets a bit too close for comfort, resist the urge to take a step back – they're simply expressing warmth and friendliness.

Now, let's talk about titles and formality. In the Spanish-speaking world, it's common to address people by their professional titles, followed by their last names. So, if you have a law degree, get ready to be called "Licenciado" or "Licenciada" – it's a sign of respect, and you've earned it.

Of course, we can't forget about the art of small talk. While discussing the weather might seem trivial, it can be a crucial icebreaker that helps you build rapport with your clients. After all, who doesn't love complaining about how unbearably hot or cold it is outside?

In short, understanding the cultural nuances of the Spanish-speaking world is an essential part of your linguistic journey. By embracing these differences and showing your clients that you respect their customs and traditions, you'll not only become a more effective communicator, but you'll also create lasting connections that transcend language barriers. So, remember: the next time you're tempted to break into a victory dance, take a moment to appreciate the wonderful world of culture that you've just stepped into. And then, by all means, dance away!

overview of the book's structure and methodology

Alright, fellow legal eagles, now that we've discussed the why and the cultural how-to, let's dive into what you can expect from this linguistic rollercoaster ride of a book. Buckle up, because we're about to embark on a whirlwind tour of our game plan for mastering legal Spanish – and trust me, it's going to be a blast!

First up, we'll tackle the foundations of the Spanish language – you know, the nuts and bolts that hold everything together. We're talking grammar, pronunciation, and all that jazz. But fear not, for we'll be guiding you through this mystical land of verbs and conjugations with the grace of a seasoned matador. Ole!

Next, we'll venture into the realm of legal vocabulary, where we'll arm you with a treasure trove of words and phrases that'll have you talking shop with your Spanish-speaking clients in no time. From the courtroom to the negotiation table, we've got you covered.

After that, we'll put your newfound knowledge to the test with some real-life dialogues and practice scenarios. Think of it as a dress rehearsal for your grand debut on the legal Spanish stage. We'll cover everything from initial consultations to cross-border negotiations, so you can confidently step into the spotlight when the time comes.

But wait, there's more! We'll also provide you with valuable resources, tips, and insights to help you continue your language-learning journey long after you've finished this book. From Spanish-language legal conferences to networking opportunities, we'll ensure that you have all the tools you need to succeed in the world of legal Spanish.

Finally, throughout this exhilarating ride, we'll be sprinkling in some cultural tidbits and anecdotes that'll not only enrich your understanding of the

Spanish-speaking world but also make for some great conversation starters at your next networking event.

So, there you have it – our master plan for turning you into a Spanish-speaking legal superstar. With a little bit of hard work, a dash of determination, and a healthy dose of humor, we'll have you dazzling your clients and colleagues with your linguistic prowess in no time. Now, let's get this fiesta started, shall we?

1 /
essential spanish grammar

basic sentence structure

ALRIGHT, amigos and amigas, let's dive headfirst into the exhilarating world of Spanish sentence structure! No need to clutch your pearls – we promise to make this journey as fun and entertaining as a night out at a salsa club. So, let's kick up our heels and explore the basic building blocks of the Spanish language.

First things first, let's talk about the Holy Trinity of sentence structure: subject, verb, and object. In Spanish, just like in English, these three amigos work together to create complete sentences. The subject is the star of the show (think: who or what the sentence is about), the verb is the action (what the subject is doing), and the object is the recipient of that action (who or what the subject is doing it to). Easy peasy, right?

Now, let's spice things up a bit. In Spanish, word order can be a tad more flexible than in English, so you can play around with the position of the subject, verb, and object to add emphasis or create a more poetic flair. For example, you might see sentences like "Los abogados ganaron el caso" (The lawyers won the case) or "El caso ganaron los abogados" (The case was won by the lawyers). Same meaning, different emphasis – it's like choosing between salsa and bachata on the dance floor.

Next up: negation. Turning a positive sentence into a negative one in Spanish is as easy as slapping a "no" in front of the verb. For example, "Los abogados ganaron el caso" (The lawyers won the case) becomes "Los abogados no ganaron el caso" (The lawyers didn't win the case). Simple, right? And no need to worry about any pesky double negatives – in Spanish, they're as welcome as an extra shot of tequila.

So, there you have it, the basics of Spanish sentence structure in a nutshell. By mastering these simple principles, you'll be well on your way to constructing your own linguistic masterpieces, from the humble "¿Dónde está el baño?" (Where's the bathroom?) to the more advanced "El juez dictaminó a favor de nuestro cliente" (The judge ruled in favor of our client). Just remember, practice makes perfect – so keep dancing your way through those Spanish sentences, and before you know it, you'll be twirling your way to fluency.

noun-adjective agreement

It's time to dive into the fabulous world of noun-adjective agreement. Now, I know what you're thinking: "Noun-adjective agreement? Sounds like the dullest party ever!" But trust me, once you get the hang of it, you'll be mixing and matching nouns and adjectives like a pro – think of it as playing dress-up with words!

In Spanish, adjectives need to agree with the nouns they modify in both gender and number. You might be wondering, "Gender? Since when do words have gender?" Well, in the Spanish language, they do – and they're quite particular about it. Nouns can be either masculine or feminine, and adjectives need to match them accordingly.

Here's the deal: most masculine adjectives end in "-o," while their feminine counterparts end in "-a." For example, "amigo" (friend) is a masculine noun, so you would use the adjective "talentoso" (talented) to describe a talented male friend. On the other hand, "amiga" is the feminine version of "friend," so you'd use "talentosa" to describe a talented female friend. Easy as pie, right?

But wait, there's more! Adjectives also need to match the number of the nouns they modify – that is, they need to be singular or plural, just like their noun partners. Simply put, if you're talking about one talented friend, you'd say "amigo talentoso" or "amiga talentosa." But if you're lucky enough to have several talented friends, you'd say "amigos talentosos" or "amigas talentosas." Just add "-s" to the adjective, and you're good to go.

Now, I know what you're thinking: "This sounds like a lot of work!" But fear not, my friend – with a bit of practice, noun-adjective agreement will become second nature. And, trust me, your Spanish-speaking clients will be impressed by your attention to detail and your impeccable grammar.

conjugating verbs

Welcome to the main event – the thrilling, spine-tingling world of conjugating verbs! Now, before you roll your eyes and groan, "Ugh, not conjugation!" let me assure you that this journey will be more like a fiesta than a snoozefest. So, grab your maracas, and let's get this verb party started!

When it comes to conjugating verbs in Spanish,

the key is understanding the three main verb groups: -ar, -er, and -ir verbs. Each group has its own unique set of endings that you'll use to conjugate the verbs in different tenses and moods. Think of it as choosing the right outfit for the right occasion – you wouldn't wear a tuxedo to a beach party, would you?

First up, we have the -ar verbs, the life of the party. To conjugate these bad boys, you'll simply remove the "-ar" ending and add the appropriate endings for each subject pronoun. For example, let's take the verb "hablar" (to talk): Yo hablo, tú hablas, él/ella habla, nosotros/nosotras hablamos, vosotros/vosotras habláis, ellos/ellas hablan. Voilà! You're now a master of -ar verb conjugation.

Next on the dance floor, we have the -er verbs, the smooth operators of the verb world. Just like with -ar verbs, you'll remove the "-er" ending and add the corresponding endings. Take "comer" (to eat) as an example: Yo como, tú comes, él/ella come, nosotros/nosotras comemos, vosotros/vosotras coméis, ellos/ellas comen. Now you're cooking with gas!

Last but not least, we have the -ir verbs, the mysterious and alluring guests at our verb fiesta. You know the drill – remove the "-ir" ending and add the appropriate endings. For instance, let's conjugate "vivir" (to live): Yo vivo, tú vives, él/ella vive, nosotros/nosotras vivimos, vosotros/vosotras vivís, ellos/ellas viven. Congratulations! You've now conquered all three verb groups.

Now, I know what you're thinking: "But what about all those irregular verbs and different tenses?" Fear not, dear reader – we'll be tackling those tricky customers in due time. For now, just revel in your newfound verb-conjugating prowess and know that you're well on your way to becoming a Spanish-speaking legal superstar.

verb tenses

Strap in for a wild ride through the wonderful world of verb tenses! Now, I know what you might be thinking: "Verb tenses? Are you kidding me? I'd rather watch paint dry." But trust me, once you've mastered these time-traveling marvels, you'll be zipping through past, present, and future like a linguistic Marty McFly. So, hop into our DeLorean and let's get this time-traveling adventure started!

First stop: the present tense. Ah, the here and now – the gift that keeps on giving. In Spanish, the present tense is your go-to for talking about actions happening right this minute, habitual actions, and general truths. Remember those -ar, -er, and -ir conjugations we discussed earlier? They'll be your best friends in the present tense. Just think of them as your trusty time-travel companions.

Next up, we're zooming back in time to the past. In Spanish, there are two main past tenses: the preterite and the imperfect. The preterite is perfect for one-time, completed actions, while the imperfect is great for ongoing or habitual past actions. Think of them as the dynamic duo of the past – together, they can paint a vivid picture of your past legal victories and courtroom dramas.

Now, let's blast off into the future! When it comes to talking about future actions in Spanish, you have a couple of options. You can use the simple future tense (with those handy -é, -ás, -á, -emos, -éis, and -án endings), or you can use the more informal "ir + a + infinitive" construction, which is like saying "going to" in English. Either way, you'll be confidently discussing future plans and legal strategies in no time.

But wait, there's more! Spanish also boasts a rich array of compound tenses, which are used to express actions that are completed or ongoing with respect to other actions. They involve the use of auxiliary verbs like "haber" (to have) and the past participle. Sounds complicated, right? But fear not, for we'll guide you through this tangled web of tenses with the grace of a salsa dancer.

pronouns and prepositions

It's time to tackle the dynamic duo of Spanish grammar: pronouns and prepositions! You might be thinking, "Pronouns and prepositions? This sounds about as exciting as a deposition on a Friday afternoon." But fear not, my friends – we're here to make this linguistic journey as entertaining as a night of karaoke with your favorite legal eagles.

Let's kick things off with pronouns. These versatile little words act as stand-ins for nouns when you want to avoid sounding like a broken record. In Spanish, you've got subject pronouns (yo, tú, él/ella, nosotros/nosotras, vosotros/vosotras, ellos/ellas), object pronouns (me, te, lo/la, nos, os, los/las), and even reflexive pronouns (me, te, se, nos, os, se). Think of them as your secret weapons for keeping your sentences fresh, snappy, and oh-so-smooth.

Now, onto the pièce de résistance: prepositions. These handy words help you show relationships between nouns, pronouns, and other words in a sentence. In Spanish, some of the most common prepositions include "de" (of, from), "a" (to, at), "en" (in, on), "con" (with), "sin" (without), and "por" (for, by). Prepositions may be small, but they pack a mighty punch – like those tiny umbrellas in your favorite tropical cocktail.

Of course, as with any language, there are some tricky aspects to pronouns and prepositions in Spanish. For example, the infamous "personal a" is a unique preposition that's used before a direct object when it's a specific person or pet. So, while you might say "Busco abogado" (I'm looking for a lawyer), you'd say "Busco a mi abogado" (I'm looking for my lawyer). It's a small touch, but it makes all the difference in sounding like a true Spanish speaker.

direct and indirect object pronouns

Gather around, dear friends, as we delve into the fascinating world of direct and indirect object pronouns! You might be thinking, "Direct and indirect object pronouns? Sounds like a snooze-fest." But have no fear – we're here to turn this grammatical adventure into a thrilling linguistic rollercoaster.

Let's start with the stars of the show: direct object pronouns. These little wonders replace the direct object of a sentence, saving you from the dreaded repetition. In Spanish, the direct object pronouns are: me, te, lo/la, nos, os, and los/las. Imagine them as your trusty sidekicks, ready to swoop in and save the day (or at least save you from sounding like a parrot).

Now, onto their equally captivating cousins: indirect object pronouns. These clever chameleons replace the indirect object in a sentence, indicating to whom or for whom an action is performed. In Spanish, the indirect object pronouns are: me, te, le, nos, os, and les. Think of them as the unsung heroes of the Spanish language, working behind the scenes to make your sentences sing.

Of course, no adventure would be complete without a challenge. In Spanish, there are instances when you need to use both direct and indirect object pronouns together in the same sentence. But don't worry – we've got you covered with a simple formula: indirect object pronoun + direct object pronoun + verb. For example, "Le doy el libro" (I give him the book) becomes "Se lo doy" (I give it to him).

And there you have it – a rip-roaring romp through the delightful realm of direct and indirect object pronouns. As you master these tiny titans of grammar, you'll find yourself weaving intricate and eloquent Spanish sentences with the skill of a master wordsmith. And who knows? You might even find yourself enjoying this linguistic escapade more than a thrilling legal thriller. ¡Hasta la próxima, amigos!

reflexive verbs

Welcome to the mesmerizing world of reflexive verbs! You might be thinking, "Reflexive verbs? Sounds as exciting as reading the fine print on a contract." But fret not, my fellow legal professionals – we're here to transform this grammar escapade into a lively linguistic adventure.

Let's start with the basics: what are reflexive verbs, anyway? Well, these charming chameleons describe actions that "reflect" back onto the subject – think of them as the boomerangs of the Spanish language. In other words, the person doing the action is also the person receiving it. For example, "me lavo" (I wash myself) or "te cepillas" (you brush yourself).

But how do you spot these linguistic gems in the wild? Simple! Reflexive verbs are often accompanied by reflexive pronouns (me, te, se, nos, os, se), which give you a helpful clue that you're dealing with a verb that's all about self-care. Just remember: subject pronoun + reflexive pronoun + verb = reflexive verb success!

Of course, no grammar adventure would be complete without a few twists and turns. In Spanish, some verbs can be both reflexive and non-reflexive, depending on the context. For example, "levantar" means "to lift," while "levantarse" means "to get up."

It's like a choose-your-own-adventure book, but with verbs!

commands

Buckle up for a thrilling ride through the world of Spanish commands! You might be thinking, "Commands? Is this a grammar lesson or a military boot camp?" But fear not, legal aficionados – we're here to make this linguistic excursion as entertaining as a night of impromptu karaoke with your law school buddies.

Commands, also known as the imperative mood, are the linguistic equivalent of bossing someone around – but in a polite and constructive way, of course. They're essential for giving instructions, making requests, or offering advice. In Spanish, commands come in all shapes and sizes, from the friendly tú form to the more formal usted and ustedes forms.

Now, let's dive into the nuts and bolts of crafting commands. For positive tú commands, you'll typically use the third person singular form of the verb in the present tense. For example, "habla" (speak) or "come" (eat). However, there are eight irregular verbs to watch out for, including "venir" (ven) and "decir" (di). Think of them as the rebellious renegades of the command world.

Negative tú commands, on the other hand, are a bit more straightforward. Simply use the present subjunctive form of the verb, like "no hables" (don't speak) or "no comas" (don't eat). For usted and ustedes commands, you'll also use the present subjunctive form, but with the appropriate subject pronoun.

But wait – there's more! We can't forget about the ever-popular nosotros commands, which are perfect for suggesting that "we" do something together, like "vámonos" (let's go) or "comamos" (let's eat). Because who doesn't love a little camaraderie in their commands?

And there you have it – an exhilarating romp through the invigorating realm of Spanish commands. As you master the art of giving instructions and offering advice in Spanish, you'll find yourself commanding the language with the finesse of a linguistic maestro. And who knows? You might even come to enjoy this grammar adventure more than a suspenseful legal thriller. ¡Adelante, amigos!

**2 /
essential legal
vocabulary**

legal terminology

ALRIGHT, esteemed colleagues, it's time to venture into the enthralling universe of Spanish legal terminology! You might be thinking, "Legal jargon in another language? This sounds about as much fun as a surprise tax audit." But worry not, my fellow legal enthusiasts – we're here to make this linguistic journey as riveting as a gripping courtroom drama.

You've undoubtedly mastered the art of legalese in English, but what about Spanish? Well, get ready to add some pizzazz to your professional vocabulary with these essential legal terms in Spanish:

1. Abogado/a: lawyer, attorney
2. Juez: judge

3. Tribunal: court
4. Contrato: contract
5. Demanda: lawsuit
6. Acusado/a: defendant
7. Querellante: plaintiff
8. Testigo: witness
9. Evidencia: evidence
10. Sentencia: verdict

But wait – there's more! As you navigate the labyrinth of Spanish legal language, you'll encounter some delightful false friends. For example, "carpeta" might sound like "carpet," but it actually means "folder." And "fianza" isn't "finance," but rather "bail" or "security deposit." Think of these linguistic curveballs as the plot twists in a thrilling legal mystery.

Of course, no legal linguistic adventure would be complete without some tongue-twisting phrases to impress your clients and colleagues. Try your hand at "presunción de inocencia" (presumption of innocence), "recusación sin causa" (peremptory challenge), or "infracción de derechos de autor" (copyright infringement). After all, who doesn't love a good linguistic challenge?

everyday vocabulary for client communication

It's time to embark on a captivating journey through the realm of everyday vocabulary for client communication in Spanish. You might be thinking, "Everyday vocabulary? I signed up for legal talk, not small talk!" But fear not – we're here to make this linguistic expedition as engaging as a gripping legal thriller.

Sure, you've got the legal terminology down, but when it comes to connecting with clients, you need more than just courtroom jargon. Let's dive into some essential conversational phrases to help you build rapport with your Spanish-speaking clients:

1. Buenos días/tardes/noches: Good morning/afternoon/night
2. Mucho gusto: Nice to meet you
3. ¿Cómo está?: How are you?
4. ¿En qué puedo ayudarle?: How can I help you?
5. Permítame revisar su caso: Let me review your case
6. Estamos trabajando en su caso: We're working on your case

7. Tenemos una actualización: We have an update
8. Vamos a necesitar más información: We'll need more information
9. Por favor, manténgame informado/a: Please keep me informed
10. Gracias por su paciencia: Thank you for your patience

But that's not all, dear colleagues! Sprinkle in some idiomatic expressions to truly shine as a Spanish-speaking legal luminary. Try out "no hay de qué" (you're welcome), "estoy a sus órdenes" (I'm at your service), or "a sus pies" (literally "at your feet," meaning at your service).

And remember, body language speaks volumes. A warm smile, a firm handshake, or a friendly nod can go a long way in building trust with your clients – no matter what language you speak.

building fluency through dialogues

initial client consultations

FASTEN YOUR SEATBELTS as we embark on a captivating voyage into the world of initial client consultations – in Spanish, no less! You might be thinking, "A consultation? This sounds as exciting as reviewing the fine print on a warranty." But fret not, my fellow law practitioners – we're here to make this linguistic journey as exhilarating as cracking open a fresh legal brief.

The initial consultation is your first opportunity to make a lasting impression on your Spanish-speaking clients. So, let's dive into some key phrases and strategies to ensure a smooth and successful first meeting:

1. Confirming the appointment: "¿Tenemos una cita hoy?" (Do we have an appointment today?)
2. Introductions: "Soy [your name], su abogado/a" (I'm [your name], your lawyer)
3. Establishing rapport: "Cuénteme un poco sobre su situación" (Tell me a bit about your situation)
4. Active listening: "Entiendo su preocupación" (I understand your concern)
5. Gathering information: "¿Puede proporcionarme más detalles?" (Can you provide more details?)
6. Discussing fees: "Nuestros honorarios son..." (Our fees are...)
7. Establishing next steps: "A continuación, vamos a..." (Next, we will...)
8. Wrapping up: "Ha sido un placer conocerle" (It's been a pleasure meeting you)

But don't stop there, dear colleagues! To truly dazzle your clients, pepper your conversation with some empathetic phrases, like "estoy aquí para ayudarle" (I'm here to help you) or "haremos todo lo posible para resolver su caso" (we'll do everything we can to resolve your case).

And let's not forget the importance of non-verbal communication. A thoughtful nod, a reassuring pat on the back, or even a well-timed furrow of the brow can speak volumes in bridging the language barrier.

case updates and strategy discussions

Grab your briefcases and dust off your legal pads as we embark on an exhilarating expedition through the realm of case updates and strategy discussions – in Spanish! You might be thinking, "Case updates? I thought this was supposed to be fun!" But fear not, my fellow legal enthusiasts – we're here to make this linguistic journey as invigorating as unearthing a groundbreaking legal precedent.

As you navigate the complex waters of case updates and strategy discussions with your Spanish-speaking clients, you'll need to master the art of clear and concise communication. Here are some key phrases and tips to help you shine like the legal luminary you are:

1. Setting the stage: "Vamos a hablar sobre su caso" (Let's talk about your case)

2. Sharing updates: "Tenemos novedades importantes" (We have important updates)
3. Discussing evidence: "Hemos encontrado nueva evidencia" (We've found new evidence)
4. Presenting options: "Existen varias opciones para abordar esta situación" (There are several options to address this situation)
5. Weighing pros and cons: "Consideremos los pros y contras" (Let's consider the pros and cons)
6. Developing a strategy: "Nuestra estrategia será..." (Our strategy will be...)
7. Setting expectations: "Es importante tener en cuenta que..." (It's important to keep in mind that...)
8. Wrapping up: "Seguiremos trabajando en su caso" (We will continue working on your case)

But wait, there's more! To truly dazzle your clients, incorporate some empathetic language, like "estamos de su lado" (we're on your side) or "confiamos en nuestro plan de acción" (we have confidence in our action plan).

And, of course, never underestimate the power of

non-verbal cues. A reassuring smile, an empathetic tilt of the head, or even a well-timed eyebrow raise can work wonders in connecting with your clients, regardless of the language barrier.

negotiations and settlements

Time to polish your negotiation skills and sharpen your strategic acumen as we venture into the exhilarating world of negotiations and settlements – in Spanish, of course! You might be thinking, "Negotiations? Can't we just hammer out a deal?" But fear not, intrepid legal practitioners – we're here to make this linguistic journey as thrilling as an unexpected courtroom twist.

When it comes to negotiations and settlements with Spanish-speaking clients, it's crucial to convey your points clearly and persuasively. So, without further ado, let's dive into some indispensable phrases and tips to make you the ultimate legal negotiator:

1. Initiating negotiations: "Es momento de comenzar las negociaciones" (It's time to start the negotiations)
2. Stating your position: "Nuestra postura es la siguiente..." (Our position is as follows...)

3. Exploring common ground: "¿En qué aspectos podemos ponernos de acuerdo?" (On what points can we agree?)
4. Making a counteroffer: "Tenemos una contraoferta para usted" (We have a counteroffer for you)
5. Handling objections: "Entendemos sus preocupaciones, pero..." (We understand your concerns, but...)
6. Emphasizing benefits: "Esta propuesta beneficia a ambas partes" (This proposal benefits both parties)
7. Reaching an agreement: "Hemos llegado a un acuerdo" (We've reached an agreement)
8. Finalizing the settlement: "Firmaremos el acuerdo de resolución" (We will sign the settlement agreement)

But that's not all, zealous legal aficionados! To truly leave your clients in awe, throw in some confidence-boosting phrases like "estamos aquí para defender sus intereses" (we're here to protect your interests) or "nuestra prioridad es encontrar la mejor solución" (our priority is finding the best solution).

And let's not forget the power of body language. A firm handshake, an assertive stance, or even a subtle nod can work wonders in making your clients feel supported and confident in your negotiation prowess.

court appearances and testimonies

Greetings, legal maestros! Ready to take center stage and bask in the spotlight? Brace yourselves for a dazzling dive into the realm of court appearances and testimonies – in Spanish, naturally! You might be thinking, "Court appearances? Where's the humor in that?" But fear not, legal virtuosos – we're here to make this linguistic odyssey as entertaining as a jaw-dropping legal plot twist.

When it comes to court appearances and testimonies with Spanish-speaking clients, precision and clarity are key. So, without further ado, let's master some crucial phrases and tips to make you the ultimate legal performer:

1. Courtroom lingo: "La sala del tribunal" (The courtroom)
2. The judge: "Su Señoría" (Your Honor)
3. The witness: "El testigo" (The witness)
4. The testimony: "El testimonio" (The testimony)
5. The evidence: "La prueba" (The evidence)
6. The objection: "¡Protesto!" (I object!)

7. The cross-examination: "El contrainterrogatorio" (The cross-examination)
8. The verdict: "El veredicto" (The verdict)

But hold your legal briefs, there's more! To truly captivate your audience (or, you know, the judge and jury), sprinkle in some empathetic phrases like "entiendo su preocupación" (I understand your concern) or "haremos todo lo posible para garantizar un resultado justo" (we will do everything possible to ensure a fair outcome).

And don't forget the power of non-verbal communication. A supportive glance, a calming hand gesture, or even a well-timed sigh can speak volumes in making your clients feel heard and understood in the courtroom.

practice scenarios and roleplays

criminal law

ARE you ready to venture into the enigmatic world of criminal law – in Spanish, of course? You might be thinking, "Criminal law? Can it be fun and lighthearted?" But rest assured, intrepid legal explorers – we're here to make this linguistic journey as engaging as a good detective novel.

When navigating the shadowy waters of criminal law with Spanish-speaking clients, it's essential to have the right terminology at your fingertips. So, without further ado, let's arm ourselves with some indispensable phrases and tips to make you the ultimate legal crime-fighter:

1. Crime: "El delito" (The crime)

2. Suspect: "El sospechoso" (The suspect)
3. Arrest: "El arresto" (The arrest)
4. Charges: "Los cargos" (The charges)
5. The accused: "El acusado" (The accused)
6. The defense: "La defensa" (The defense)
7. The prosecutor: "El fiscal" (The prosecutor)
8. The sentence: "La sentencia" (The sentence)

But that's not all, eager legal adventurers! To truly impress your clients, pepper your speech with empathetic phrases like "estamos aquí para proteger sus derechos" (we're here to protect your rights) or "trabajaremos incansablemente para lograr un resultado favorable" (we will work tirelessly to achieve a favorable outcome).

And let's not underestimate the impact of body language. A reassuring nod, a confident stance, or even a well-timed raised eyebrow can make all the difference in putting your clients at ease and making them feel supported.

civil law

Are you ready to dive into the vast ocean of civil law – in Spanish, of course? You might be wondering, "Civil law? Can it be entertaining?" Fear not, intrepid legal explorers – we're here to make this linguistic journey as delightful as a well-argued legal debate.

When navigating the intricate world of civil law with Spanish-speaking clients, it's essential to be equipped with the right terminology. So, let's equip ourselves with some indispensable phrases and tips to make you the ultimate legal negotiator:

1. Contract: "El contrato" (The contract)
2. Plaintiff: "El demandante" (The plaintiff)
3. Defendant: "El demandado" (The defendant)
4. Damages: "Los daños" (The damages)
5. Settlement: "El acuerdo" (The settlement)
6. Mediation: "La mediación" (The mediation)
7. Arbitration: "El arbitraje" (The arbitration)
8. Litigation: "El litigio" (The litigation)

But wait, there's more, legal adventurers! To truly connect with your clients, sprinkle in some empathetic phrases like "entendemos lo importante que es resolver este conflicto" (we understand how important it is to resolve this conflict) or "haremos todo lo posible para lograr el mejor resultado posible" (we'll do everything possible to achieve the best possible outcome).

And let's not forget the power of body language.

A warm smile, a reassuring pat on the shoulder, or even a well-timed eyebrow waggle can work wonders in making your clients feel heard and understood.

family law

Are you prepared to delve into the intricate maze of family law – in Spanish, of course? You might be pondering, "Family law? Can it be engaging?" Rest assured, intrepid legal explorers – we're here to make this linguistic journey as captivating as a telenovela.

When navigating the complex world of family law with Spanish-speaking clients, it's essential to master the right terminology. So, let's gather some indispensable phrases and tips to make you the ultimate legal advocate for families:

1. Marriage: "El matrimonio" (The marriage)
2. Divorce: "El divorcio" (The divorce)
3. Custody: "La custodia" (The custody)
4. Child support: "La manutención de los hijos" (The child support)
5. Alimony: "La pensión alimenticia" (The alimony)
6. Adoption: "La adopción" (The adoption)

7. Prenuptial agreement: "El acuerdo prenupcial" (The prenuptial agreement)
8. Visitation rights: "Los derechos de visita" (The visitation rights)

But hold on, legal adventurers! To truly resonate with your clients, incorporate empathetic phrases like "estamos aquí para apoyar a su familia durante estos momentos difíciles" (we're here to support your family during these challenging times) or "trabajaremos juntos para encontrar la mejor solución para todos" (we'll work together to find the best solution for everyone).

And let's not underestimate the influence of body language. A comforting nod, a gentle touch on the arm, or even an appropriately timed wink can make a world of difference in helping your clients feel cared for and understood.

immigration law

Are you ready to dive into the vast ocean of immigration law, all while learning Spanish? We promise this linguistic adventure will be as riveting as an international spy thriller, complete with twists, turns, and a bit of laughter.

Navigating the intricacies of immigration law

requires a solid grasp of legal terms, along with the ability to communicate effectively with your Spanish-speaking clients. So, let's gather some indispensable phrases and tips that will have you feeling like the James Bond of immigration law:

1. Visa: "La visa" (The visa)
2. Green card: "La tarjeta verde" (The green card)
3. Deportation: "La deportación" (The deportation)
4. Asylum: "El asilo" (The asylum)
5. Work permit: "El permiso de trabajo" (The work permit)
6. Citizenship: "La ciudadanía" (The citizenship)
7. Adjustment of status: "El ajuste de estatus" (The adjustment of status)
8. Consular processing: "El proceso consular" (The consular processing)

But wait, there's more! To truly connect with your clients, sprinkle in some empathetic phrases, such as "entendemos lo complicado que puede ser el proceso migratorio" (we understand how complicated the immigration process can be) or "nuestro objetivo es ayudarle a alcanzar sus sueños" (our goal is to help you achieve your dreams).

And let's not forget the power of nonverbal communication. A reassuring smile, a firm handshake, or a knowing glance can work wonders in putting your clients at ease.

There you have it – a gripping adventure through the exhilarating world of immigration law in Spanish. As you tackle these linguistic challenges, you'll become an unstoppable force in the quest to help clients navigate the complexities of immigration. And who knows, maybe you'll even uncover the secret to making immigration law an edge-of-your-seat experience. ¡Hasta la próxima, futuros expertos en leyes migratorias!

spanish language resources

recommended spanish-english legal dictionaries

ARE you feeling like a kid in a candy store, eager to gobble up all the Spanish legal jargon you can find? Well, look no further! We've handpicked a scrumptious selection of Spanish-English legal dictionaries that will transform you into a bilingual legal superhero, cape and all.

1. "Diccionario Jurídico Español-Inglés, Inglés-Español" by Steven M. Kaplan – This dictionary has all the bells and whistles. It's like the Batmobile of legal dictionaries, filled with thousands of

entries, sample sentences, and even specialized vocabulary for different areas of law. In no time, you'll be well on your way to saving the world – one legal term at a time.

2. "Diccionario de Términos Jurídicos: Inglés-Español, Spanish-English" by Enrique Alcaraz Varó and Brian Hughes – This dynamic duo of a dictionary is like a trusty sidekick, always ready to provide backup with over 20,000 entries, pronunciation guides, and helpful explanations of legal concepts. You'll never feel like you're facing linguistic challenges alone with this trusty companion by your side.

3. "Diccionario Bilingüe de Terminología Jurídica: Español-Inglés, Inglés-Español" by Maria Isabel Orrego Rodas – Imagine you're trapped in a maze of complex legal language. This dictionary is like a trusty compass guiding you through the labyrinth, thanks to its easy-to-understand explanations and concise definitions. You'll emerge victorious on the other side, ready to tackle any legal case that comes your way.

4. "Black's Law Dictionary" – Last but not least, the pièce de résistance of legal dictionaries. While not specifically Spanish-English, this classic dictionary includes many Spanish legal terms and phrases, making it an essential part of any legal professional's arsenal. Think of it as your utility belt, packed with everything you need to conquer the world of law.

online language-learning platforms

Are you ready to embark on a quest to find the most marvelous Spanish-English legal dictionaries? Buckle up, because we're about to explore a treasure trove of resources that will transform you into a polyglot paralegal or a bilingual barrister in no time!

1. "Diccionario Jurídico Español-Inglés, Inglés-Español" by Steven M. Kaplan – This is the dictionary equivalent of a superhero, cape and all. It's jam-packed with thousands of entries, example sentences, and specialized vocabulary for various areas of law. You'll be soaring through the legal skies in style with this trusty tome at your side.

2. "Diccionario de Términos Jurídicos: Inglés-Español, Spanish-English" by Enrique Alcaraz Varó and Brian Hughes – Imagine a dictionary that's as loyal as a well-trained sidekick. With over 20,000 entries, pronunciation guides, and helpful explanations of legal concepts, this dynamic duo of a dictionary has your back, come rain or shine.

3. "Diccionario Bilingüe de Terminología Jurídica: Español-Inglés, Inglés-Español" by Maria Isabel Orrego Rodas – Think of this dictionary as your personal GPS, navigating you through the winding roads of complex legal language. Its easy-to-understand explanations and concise definitions will keep you on track, ready to tackle any legal case that comes your way.

4. "Black's Law Dictionary" – Last but not least, the crown jewel of legal dictionaries. Though not exclusively Spanish-English, this classic dictionary includes a plethora of Spanish legal terms and phrases, making it an indispensable part of any legal professional's collection. Picture it as a Swiss Army knife, equipped with

everything you need to triumph in the world of law.

legal document translation services

Psst! Are you ready for a secret weapon that'll knock the socks off your legal opponents? Look no further than legal document translation services. These linguistic superheroes swoop in and save the day when your language skills are a tad, shall we say, shaky.

1. TransPerfect - These folks are practically language wizards. With their highly skilled translators and rigorous quality control, TransPerfect will take your legal documents and transform them into crystal-clear Spanish prose that even Don Quixote would envy.
2. ProZ - A bustling online marketplace where you can connect with freelance translators who have been vetted by their peers. Think of it as the Wild West of translation, but with a more refined touch. Giddy up, partner!
3. Gengo - Are you in need of a translation that's faster than a speeding bullet?

Gengo's got your back. Their expert translators will have your legal documents translated quicker than you can say "E pluribus unum."

4. Marsolutions - With a name like Marsolutions, you'd expect them to provide translations that are out of this world. And you'd be right! Their expert team of legal translators will make your documents sparkle with linguistic finesse.

5. Day Translations - When you need a translation that's as accurate as a laser-guided missile, Day Translations is the way to go. Their certified translators will ensure your legal documents are pitch-perfect and ready for the courtroom.

language exchange and practice groups

Once upon a time, in a world brimming with eager language learners, there existed a secret society of knowledge-seekers who gathered to share their linguistic wisdom. Okay, it's not really a secret society, but it's still pretty cool. Behold the wondrous realm of language exchange and practice groups!

1. Tandem - Think of Tandem as a modern-day linguistic Noah's Ark, where language partners come in pairs. Find a buddy who speaks the language you're learning and who wants to learn yours. Voilà! A match made in heaven.

2. ConversationExchange - It's like speed dating, but for language learners! Meet other polyglots, practice your speaking skills, and expand your vocabulary at lightning speed. No more awkward silences, just linguistic nirvana.

3. Meetup - Want to socialize and learn at the same time? Meetup is the place to be. Discover local language practice groups and immerse yourself in a melting pot of linguistic goodness. Who knows, you might even make some new friends along the way!

4. MyLanguageExchange - Picture this: a digital playground where you can frolic in the fields of foreign phrases and grammar rules. MyLanguageExchange is an online platform where you can chat with language enthusiasts from all over the world. It's like having a global pen pal with benefits (language benefits, that is).

5. iTalki - Ready to take your language skills to the next level? iTalki connects you with professional language tutors for one-on-one lessons, ensuring that you get the personalized attention you need to master the linguistic arts.

cultural insights and tips

understanding hispanic culture and customs

ROLL OUT THE RED CARPET, because we're about to embark on a whirlwind tour of Hispanic culture and customs! Buckle up, because this linguistic roller coaster is full of twists, turns, and tantalizing tidbits.

1. Holy guacamole, it's all about family! Hispanic culture places a strong emphasis on close-knit families and extended relatives. So, when you're invited to a family gathering, be prepared to meet everyone from abuelita to the family dog. And remember, blood is thicker than agua.

2. Food glorious food! Did someone say tacos? In Hispanic culture, meals are a time for bonding and celebration. Whether it's a festive feast or a simple snack, food is a symbol of love and togetherness. Be prepared for a smorgasbord of flavors, textures, and spice levels that'll make your taste buds dance a salsa!

3. Time is relative, my friends. In many Hispanic countries, punctuality is, well, not exactly top priority. So, if your dinner invitation says 7 p.m., don't be surprised if the party doesn't start until 8 or even 9. Just embrace the flexible timeframe and enjoy the ride!

4. Personal space? What's that? Hispanic cultures tend to be warm and expressive, with plenty of hugs, cheek kisses, and hearty handshakes. Remember, there's no such thing as too close for comfort when it comes to making connections. So, let your guard down and embrace the love!

5. Fiesta, siesta, repeat! Celebrations and festivals abound in Hispanic culture, so you're bound to stumble upon a colorful parade, religious procession, or lively street party during your linguistic

journey. Don your dancing shoes and prepare to immerse yourself in a vibrant world of music, laughter, and joy.

By diving headfirst into Hispanic culture and customs, you'll not only enrich your language skills but also gain a deeper appreciation for the beauty and diversity of this amazing community. So, go forth and explore, oh intrepid linguist, and let the spirit of Hispanic heritage light your way!

addressing clients with respect and formality

In this exhilarating escapade, we'll explore the ins and outs of proper client etiquette while keeping things light and breezy. So, grab your top hat and cane, and let's waltz our way through this linguistic ballroom!

1. The name game: In many cultures, addressing someone by their first name can be a tad too familiar. Instead, opt for the more formal route by using their last name with a title, such as Señor García or Señora Pérez. This simple switcharoo

demonstrates that you value their dignity and respect their position.

2. The magic words: Please, thank you, and you're welcome – these age-old phrases are like the secret sauce of politeness. While they might seem like no-brainers, these gems can add a touch of grace and courtesy to your interactions. So, liberally sprinkle your conversations with por favor, gracias, and de nada to keep things classy.

3. A firm handshake and eye contact: When meeting a client for the first time, a confident handshake and steady eye contact can work wonders in establishing trust and rapport. Plus, it sets the stage for a professional relationship that's built on mutual respect and admiration.

4. Mind your manners: In the legal world, decorum is the name of the game. Whether you're drafting a letter, sending an email, or having a face-to-face chat, always strive for politeness, clarity, and professionalism. A well-placed "I hope this message finds you well" or "I appreciate your time and consideration" can work wonders in fostering a positive relationship with your client.

5. Adiós with style: When bidding farewell to
   a client, always do so with grace and
   warmth. A simple "it was a pleasure to
   meet you" or "thank you for your time" can
   leave a lasting impression and pave the
   way for future interactions.

By mastering the art of addressing clients with respect and formality, you'll not only elevate your communication skills but also earn the admiration of your esteemed clientele.

avoiding language pitfalls and misunderstandings

In this thrilling linguistic adventure, we'll help you sidestep any language pitfalls and misunderstandings that might make your legal journey a little less, well, explosive. Strap on your language-proof vest, and let's dive into the wild world of communication faux pas!

1. Double-check those double meanings:
   Some words in Spanish might sound like
   English words, but they can have entirely
   different meanings. Take "embarazada" for
   example – it means "pregnant," not

"embarrassed." Yikes! Save yourself from awkward situations by double-checking those tricky words before you use them.

2. Slow your roll: When speaking with clients who aren't native English speakers, it's easy to get carried away and start speaking at lightning speed. Slow down, take a breath, and enunciate each word clearly. You'll be doing both you and your client a favor, making sure that important information doesn't get lost in translation.

3. Regional slang: Be mindful of slang and colloquial expressions that may not be universally understood. Stick to standard Spanish and avoid using jargon or idioms that might leave your client more perplexed than a three-legged llama at a hoedown.

4. The fine art of listening: Sometimes, misunderstandings stem from simply not paying enough attention to what the other person is saying. Practice active listening, and make sure you fully understand your client's needs and concerns. You'll not only avoid miscommunication but also build a stronger rapport with your clients.

5. When in doubt, ask: If you're unsure about a word, phrase, or concept, don't be afraid to ask your client for clarification. It's better to ask and learn than to assume and make a potentially costly mistake. Plus, your clients will appreciate your diligence and commitment to understanding their needs.

By following these tips, you'll be well on your way to sidestepping language pitfalls and avoiding misunderstandings like a linguistic ninja. After all, clear communication is key to providing top-notch legal services – and keeping your clients smiling, rather than scratching their heads in confusion!

building confidence in legal spanish

strategies for vocabulary retention and recall

AND NOW, dear reader, we shall embark on an epic quest to conquer the seemingly unconquerable: vocabulary retention and recall. Fear not, for we shall emerge victorious, armed with an arsenal of foolproof strategies that would make even the most valiant of knights green with envy. So, gird your mental loins and join us on this noble crusade!

1. The almighty flashcard: This humble, unassuming tool has been the trusty sidekick of language learners for generations. Create flashcards with Spanish words on one side and their

English translations on the other. Review them regularly, and before you know it, those pesky new words will be firmly entrenched in your memory.

2. The power of association: Build a mental bridge between new words and familiar images, feelings, or experiences. For example, if you're learning the word "pájaro" (bird), picture a bird perched on your windowsill, serenading you with a delightful morning song. The stronger and more vivid the connection, the better your recall will be!

3. The great repetition game: Studies show that repeating new information at regular intervals helps strengthen memory. So, go ahead and repeat those new words to yourself throughout the day – while brushing your teeth, commuting to work, or cooking dinner. Sure, you might get some strange looks, but who cares? You're on a quest, after all!

4. The mnemonic magic: Create catchy mnemonics to help remember new words. For example, to remember "cuchillo" (knife), you could think of a cook who says, "Ouch! Eeyore!" when she

accidentally cuts herself. Get creative, and don't be afraid to be a little silly. The weirder the mnemonic, the easier it is to remember!

5. The challenge of context: Use new words in sentences to help cement their meaning in your mind. Engage in conversations, write stories, or even compose ditties using the words you're trying to learn. The more you practice using the words in context, the better you'll be at remembering them when it really counts.

Fearlessly employing these strategies, you shall emerge victorious from the battlefield of vocabulary retention and recall, your memory brimming with newfound linguistic prowess.

improving listening comprehension

Ah, listening comprehension – the bane of many a language learner's existence. But fear not, intrepid adventurer, for we have some tricks up our sleeves that'll have you deciphering the melodious sounds of Spanish in no time. Ready? Let's dive into the cacophony of linguistic delights that await!

1. Tune in to the sweet sounds of Spanish: Surround yourself with the harmonious notes of Spanish by listening to podcasts, watching movies, and catching some telenovelas. It's like being serenaded by a chorus of angels, except these angels are teaching you legal terminology.

2. Slow and steady wins the race: When you're starting out, it can feel like native speakers are engaged in a high-speed race to the finish line. Don't panic! Look for resources with slowed-down audio, so you can catch your breath and really savor each word. Eventually, you'll be able to keep up with the big leagues.

3. Eavesdrop like a pro: When you're out and about, keep an ear out for Spanish speakers. Pretend you're a secret agent on a mission to gather intel (strictly for educational purposes, of course). The more you practice tuning in to real-life conversations, the better your listening comprehension will become.

4. Embrace the power of transcription: Choose a short audio clip and try to transcribe it word for word. Then, compare your transcription to the original transcript

(if available) or a trusted translation. This exercise will sharpen your listening skills faster than a quick-witted comedian can deliver a punchline.

5. The granddaddy of all tips: Practice, practice, and then practice some more! Like a fine wine, your listening skills will only improve with time and experience. So, be patient, and soon enough, you'll be navigating the mellifluous world of Spanish with the grace of a linguistic swan.

By following these sage tips, your listening comprehension will soar to new heights, and you'll be the envy of all your fellow Spanish learners.

enhancing speaking proficiency

Here, you'll learn to tame the wild and rambunctious beast that is the Spanish language and mold it into a well-behaved, eloquent companion. So, buckle up, and let's embark on this exhilarating journey together!

1. Mirror, mirror on the wall: It's time for some one-on-one practice with your favorite conversation partner – you! Chat

with yourself in the mirror, narrating your day or discussing your latest legal triumph. It may feel a bit silly, but it's a judgment-free way to practice and boost your confidence.

2. The pen is mightier than the sword: Prepare for linguistic battle by honing your verbal skills through writing. Jot down your thoughts, legal arguments, or even grocery lists in Spanish. This will reinforce the connection between thought and speech, turning you into a verbal Spanish ninja in no time.

3. A friend indeed: Seek out Spanish-speaking pals and engage in conversation with them. Whether you meet in person, join an online language exchange, or chat with your abuela, the more you practice with real people, the better your speaking skills will become. Plus, you'll make some new amigos along the way!

4. Record yourself, superstar: Unleash your inner diva and record yourself speaking Spanish. Then, listen back and critique your performance. It's like being your own personal Simon Cowell, but with fewer

scathing remarks and more helpful feedback.

5. Embrace the stutter: Like a baby learning to walk, you'll stumble and stutter your way through your first few conversations. Don't be disheartened! Embrace your linguistic faux pas, and use them as an opportunity to learn and grow. Soon, you'll be strutting down the Spanish-speaking runway with finesse and style.

With these trusty tips by your side, you'll be well on your way to conquering the art of Spanish-speaking proficiency. Go forth, brave linguist, and dazzle the world with your newfound oratory skills!

embracing a growth mindset

Gather 'round, noble adventurers, as we venture into the enchanted land of growth mindset! This magical realm, discovered by the wise sorceress Carol Dweck, will reveal to you the secrets of self-improvement and boundless linguistic prowess.

1. The Power of "Yet": Behold, the simple, humble word "yet," with the strength to transform your outlook on learning! When

faced with a challenge or a mistake, instead of saying, "I can't do it," add "yet" to the end – "I can't do it, yet." This tiny word packs a powerful punch and reminds you that with effort, you'll soon conquer that pesky Spanish subjunctive.

2. The Art of Constructive Criticism: When feedback is given, instead of shrugging it off or taking it personally, embrace it as a golden ticket to self-improvement. Remember, even the most skilled linguists once stumbled through their first conversations. Transform critiques into valuable lessons, and watch your Spanish skills soar!

3. The Mighty Mountain of Mistakes: Mistakes are like a mountain: you have to climb them to reach the peak of success. Embrace errors as an inevitable part of your journey and use them as a stepping stone to greatness. The more mistakes you make, the closer you'll be to becoming the Spanish-speaking hero you were destined to be.

4. The Quest for Knowledge: Always be curious, intrepid explorer! Seek out new words, grammar rules, and cultural tidbits.

Whether you stumble upon a mysterious legal term or a new regional slang, treasure every discovery as a valuable addition to your ever-growing trove of knowledge.

5. The Wizardry of Persistence: Finally, harness the power of persistence. Like a tenacious wizard casting spells, practice and persevere until you perfect your linguistic sorcery. Remember, Rome wasn't built in a day, and neither is Spanish fluency!

And so, dear adventurer, as you embark on your quest to conquer the Spanish language, remember to embrace the growth mindset and trust in its magical powers. With this enchanted elixir by your side, you'll soon be fluent enough to charm the socks off even the most stoic of Spanish-speaking legal eagles. Good luck, and may the growth mindset be with you!

legal writing and document review in spanish

tips for effective legal writing in spanish

WELL, well, well! If it isn't the aspiring legal maestro, eager to craft some magnificent Spanish prose! Fear not, for I shall bestow upon you the sacred knowledge of effective legal writing in Spanish. Behold, the mystic tips that shall guide your quill (or keyboard) to produce eloquent and persuasive legal documents:

1. Precision is key: As a master chef knows, a pinch of salt can make or break a dish. Likewise, in legal writing, precision is everything. Choose your words with care, ensuring that each one accurately conveys

your intended meaning. Like a bullseye in darts, aim for the exact target and watch your argument land flawlessly.

2. The power of structure: Just as a solid foundation is crucial for a sturdy building, a well-organized structure is essential for clear legal writing. Begin with a strong introduction, followed by logical, coherent paragraphs that support your argument. Finally, wrap up with a compelling conclusion that ties it all together like a neatly wrapped present.

3. The magic of brevity: Why use ten words when one will do? Like a minimalist artist, paint your masterpiece using only the most essential strokes. Eliminate unnecessary words and phrases, and watch as your prose becomes more powerful and persuasive.

4. The elegance of clarity: Legal documents can be complex, but that doesn't mean your writing should be. Strive for clarity and simplicity in your language, ensuring that even the most complex concepts are easily understood. Remember, a spoonful of clarity helps the legal jargon go down!

5. The art of persuasion: As a legal writing virtuoso, your aim is to persuade your reader. To achieve this, wield the mighty sword of logic, present irrefutable evidence, and eloquently address potential counterarguments. With these tools in hand, you'll have your reader nodding in agreement before they even know what hit them.

6. The triumph of proofreading: Before you release your written magnum opus into the world, give it one final polish. Review your work with a critical eye, fixing any errors in grammar, punctuation, or syntax. Remember, a flawless legal document is like a well-tailored suit, inspiring confidence and admiration in all who behold it.

reviewing and understanding spanish legal documents

You've ventured deep into the realm of Spanish legal documents, have you? Fear not, brave explorer, for I shall be your trusty guide through the dense jungle of legalese. Together, we shall navigate the twists and turns of legal syntax, and you will emerge triumphant, armed with the knowledge you need to dissect and understand even the most formidable Spanish legal documents. Onward!

1. The compass of context: When deciphering a legal document, context is everything. Just as a wayward traveler relies on their trusty compass to find their bearings, you must use the context of the document to guide your understanding. Look for clues within the text itself – what is the purpose of the document, who are the parties involved, and what are the main issues being addressed?

2. The machete of familiarity: To cut through the dense underbrush of legal jargon, you must first become familiar with the terms and phrases commonly used in Spanish legal documents. Start by learning the key words specific to the area of law in question. With practice, you'll be able to slice through legalese like butter!

3. The map of structure: Legal documents can be labyrinthine, with clauses and subclauses snaking around every corner. To make sense of it all, study the structure of the document. Identify headings and

subheadings, and take note of how the document is organized. With a solid grasp of the structure, you'll be better equipped to navigate the maze of legal text.

4. The magnifying glass of attention to detail: Legal documents are chock-full of fine print, and it's crucial that you don't miss a single word. So, whip out your metaphorical magnifying glass, and scrutinize each and every sentence. Pay special attention to dates, deadlines, and any terms that carry legal consequences.

5. The life raft of professional help: Sometimes, even the most intrepid legal document explorer needs a helping hand. If you find yourself lost in a sea of legal jargon, don't hesitate to consult a trusted bilingual attorney or a legal translator. They'll help you stay afloat and ensure that you understand the document in its entirety.

6. The treasure chest of practice: Finally, remember that practice makes perfect! The more you immerse yourself in Spanish legal documents, the better equipped you'll be to tackle even the most complex cases. So, dive in, and with time, you'll find

yourself navigating the world of Spanish legal documents with ease and confidence.

drafting bilingual legal documents

You've decided to don your linguistic superhero cape and embark on the thrilling adventure of drafting bilingual legal documents. Fear not, for I am here to impart my wisdom and guide you through this exhilarating quest. With great power comes great responsibility, so let's get you ready to save the day in not just one, but two languages!

Step 1: Know your terrain

Before you set out on your mission, familiarize yourself with the legal systems and terminology of both languages. Keep in mind that some concepts may not have direct translations, so be prepared to explain or adapt them accordingly.

Step 2: The power of parallelism

Embrace the power of parallelism by drafting both language versions side by side. This will not only help you maintain consistency, but also make it easier to spot any discrepancies between the two texts.

Step 3: The art of adaptation

Translating legal documents is no walk in the park, and you may need to adapt certain phrases or concepts to suit the target language. Remember, your goal is to ensure that the meaning is preserved, even if it requires some creative linguistic acrobatics.

Step 4: Stay in sync

When drafting bilingual documents, it's crucial to ensure that both language versions remain in sync. Double-check that all dates, deadlines, and important terms match up perfectly between the two versions.

Step 5: Mind the gaps

When translating complex legal concepts, you might encounter some gaps between the languages. In such cases, consider adding explanatory footnotes to clarify any ambiguities or discrepancies.

Step 6: Assemble your dream team

In the world of bilingual legal drafting, two heads are often better than one. Collaborate with a colleague or seek the help of a professional legal translator to make sure your document is as accurate and comprehensive as possible.

Step 7: Proofread, proofread, proofread!

Nobody's perfect, not even superheroes. So, before you send your bilingual masterpiece out into the world, make sure you've proofread it thoroughly. Spelling mistakes and grammatical errors can weaken your legal Kryptonite, so take the time to polish your work to perfection.

9 /
advanced legal
spanish topics

latin american legal systems and their distinctions

ROLL UP, roll up, and get ready to embark on a thrilling journey through the diverse legal landscapes of Latin America! Brace yourselves, intrepid explorers, as we traverse this vast region and uncover the fascinating distinctions between its various legal systems. Buckle up, because it's going to be a wild ride!

First stop: The Majestic Andes of Civil Law

In the highlands of Latin America, you'll find that most countries operate under civil law systems, with roots stretching back to the towering peaks of ancient Roman law. Here, you'll encounter comprehensive legal codes that govern the land, covering everything from property disputes to tort law. Remember, though, no two civil law systems are exactly alike, so tread carefully as you navigate these mountainous terrains.

Next up: The Exotic Jungles of Common Law

Venture deep into the lush jungles of Belize and Guyana, where you'll discover the only two Latin American countries that follow common law systems. Much like the wild flora and fauna of these tropical rainforests, common law in these lands has evolved over time through the organic process of judicial decisions and precedent-setting cases. So, be prepared to get up close and personal with some legal wildlife!

Onward to the Mesmerizing Deserts of Mixed Legal Systems

As we journey through the arid expanses of Latin America, we stumble upon a fascinating hybrid: countries like Bolivia, Ecuador, and Paraguay, where elements of both civil and customary law coexist. In these legal oases, you'll find a fascinating fusion of ancient customs and modern legislation, making for a truly captivating legal adventure.

Behold the Volcanic Islands of Legal Reform

Finally, let's set sail to the volcanic islands of legal reform, where the legal landscape is ever-changing and dynamic. Across Latin America, you'll find countries in various stages of transformation, implementing reforms to their legal systems in response to shifting social, political, and economic landscapes. Keep an eye out for emerging trends and innovations as you traverse these legal hotspots.

And there you have it, explorers – a whirlwind tour of Latin America's diverse legal systems and their unique distinctions. As you continue your legal adventures in this vibrant region, we hope you'll come to appreciate the rich tapestry of legal traditions and customs that shape the way justice is pursued and upheld. Happy exploring!

navigating cultural nuances in international legal settings

Now we embark on an expedition into the fascinating world of cultural nuances in international legal settings. So, dust off your diplomatic passports and let's set sail into the uncharted waters of cross-cultural communication. Bon voyage!

To begin, we must dive into the deep ocean of body language. You may find yourself swimming amongst the sharks of miscommunication if you're not careful! For instance, maintaining eye contact could be interpreted as a sign of respect and attentiveness in one culture, while in another, it might be seen as a challenge or an invasion of personal space. So, keep your eyes peeled and your fins at the ready, and remember to tread lightly in these delicate waters.

Next, let's climb the mountain of verbal communication. Scaling these linguistic peaks can be a perilous task, as every culture has its unique ways of expressing politeness, respect, and even disagreement. Sometimes, it's not what you say, but how you say it that matters most. Be mindful of the tone, formality, and manner in which you speak, and always be prepared for the unexpected gusts of idiomatic expressions that might blow you off course.

Now, we venture into the dense jungle of gift-giving customs. Gifts can be tokens of gratitude, respect, or even friendship, but beware, for they can also be laden with hidden meanings and potential pitfalls. In some cultures, the act of gift-giving is imbued with great symbolic importance, while in others, it's a simple gesture of goodwill. Tread carefully through this tangled web of customs and avoid the poisonous plants of offense.

As we cross the vast desert of punctuality, remember that time is a relative concept. While punctuality may be highly valued in some cultures, it might not hold the same weight in others. To avoid getting lost in the sands of misunderstandings, always be prepared to adapt your expectations and demonstrate flexibility when it comes to matters of time.

Finally, we reach the glittering city of professional attire. The way you dress can speak volumes about your intentions, professionalism, and even your cultural sensitivity. When entering the realm of international legal settings, make sure to pack a wardrobe suitable for various occasions – from the formal black-tie events to the more casual networking receptions.

And there you have it, dear travelers! A thrilling journey through the diverse landscape of cultural nuances in international legal settings. As you continue to explore this fascinating world, may you always remember to embrace the spirit of adventure, respect, and adaptability, and never forget that the true treasure lies in the rich tapestry of human experiences that connect us all. Happy navigating!

continuing education and professional development

spanish-language legal conferences and seminars

STRAP on your seatbelts and fasten your thinking caps, because we're about to embark on a thrilling ride through the exhilarating terrain of Spanish-language legal conferences and seminars. Are you ready for the intellectual rollercoaster of a lifetime? Then let's go!

First stop: the majestic land of networking opportunities. At these conferences and seminars, you'll have the unique chance to rub elbows with legal experts from across the Spanish-speaking globe. Mingle with your fellow legal eagles, exchange business cards, and forge alliances that will last a lifetime. Just remember to keep your wits about you and always be ready with a witty icebreaker or two – who knows, you might just charm your way into a new collaboration or mentorship!

Next up: the stimulating realm of knowledge acquisition. Spanish-language legal conferences and seminars are a veritable treasure trove of cutting-edge information, invaluable insights, and thought-provoking discussions. Prepare to have your mind blown as you delve into the latest developments in your niche practice area, or even venture into uncharted territories to expand your legal horizons. The possibilities for growth and learning are truly endless!

Now, let's take a detour through the enchanting forest of professional development. These events are the perfect opportunity to sharpen your skills, refine your techniques, and hone your craft to a razor-sharp edge. Whether it's through workshops, interactive sessions, or hands-on demonstrations, you'll be sure to walk away with a wealth of new tools and strategies to level up your legal game.

Finally, we arrive at the dazzling city of inspiration and motivation. At these Spanish-language legal conferences and seminars, you'll have the chance to hear from some of the brightest minds and most innovative thinkers in the legal world. From keynote speeches to panel discussions, these events are designed to spark your creativity, fuel your passion, and reignite your commitment to the noble pursuit of justice.

study abroad and language immersion programs

Well, well, well, if it isn't the intrepid language enthusiasts seeking to dive headfirst into the deep end of linguistic immersion! Fear not, brave souls, for you have come to the right place! We're about to embark on a thrilling odyssey through the wonders of study abroad and language immersion programs. Buckle up, amigos, and let's get this show on the road!

Picture this: you, a courageous language learner, find yourself strolling down the picturesque streets of a quaint Spanish village, savoring churros at a local café, or haggling with street vendors in the bustling heart of Mexico City. This, my friends, is the stuff language dreams are made of, and it's all within your reach through the magic of study abroad and language immersion programs.

Think of it like a choose-your-own-adventure story, where you get to handpick the backdrop for your linguistic escapades. Whether you fancy the sun-soaked beaches of Spain, the majestic mountains of Argentina, or the vibrant cityscapes of Colombia, the world is your oyster, and the pearl within is fluency in the beautiful Spanish language.

But wait, there's more! Not only do these programs provide the ultimate immersive experience, but they also come with a heaping side order of cultural enlightenment. You'll have the opportunity to soak up the customs, traditions, and idiosyncrasies of your chosen destination, all while forging lifelong friendships with fellow language aficionados and local residents alike.

As for the pièce de résistance, these programs often come equipped with top-notch teachers and tailored curricula to accelerate your language progress at warp speed. You'll be conjugating verbs, mastering subjunctives, and tossing around legal jargon like a seasoned pro in no time!

networking with spanish-speaking legal professionals

Alright, all you charismatic legal eagles, it's time to talk about something near and dear to our hearts: networking with Spanish-speaking legal professionals! Because, let's face it, we all know that the real secret sauce to success in the legal world is not just what you know, but who you know. Am I right or am I right? So, let's get to mingling, shall we?

Now, I know what you're thinking: "But how do I even begin to break the ice with these esteemed Spanish-speaking legal wizards?" Fear not, my friends, for I have some foolproof tips to turn you into a networking maestro in no time!

First things first, let's talk about social media. Yes, that's right, even the most distinguished of legal professionals can't resist the siren call of LinkedIn, Twitter, and the like. So, polish up your profiles, add some bilingual flair, and start connecting with your future amigos in the legal world!

And speaking of online platforms, don't forget about the treasure trove of virtual networking events, webinars, and forums where you can rub virtual elbows with the crème de la crème of Spanish-speaking legal professionals. Just remember to practice your elevator pitch and have a snazzy digital business card at the ready!

But let's not neglect the tried-and-true method of good old-fashioned face-to-face networking. Whenever you find yourself at a conference, seminar, or even a casual social gathering, be on the lookout for opportunities to strike up a conversation with your fellow Spanish-speaking legal enthusiasts. A well-timed joke or anecdote can work wonders in breaking the ice and forging new connections.

Of course, we can't forget the importance of maintaining these relationships once you've built them. Keep the lines of communication open, share relevant articles or updates, and don't be afraid to reach out for advice or insights from your ever-growing network of Spanish-speaking legal contacts. After all, you've worked hard to establish these connections, so why not make the most of them?

opportunities for pro bono work in spanish-speaking communities

Attention, all you kind-hearted legal aficionados! We're about to dive into the wonderfully fulfilling world of pro bono work in Spanish-speaking communities. That's right, my justice-seeking friends, it's time to put your skills to good use and make a difference in the lives of those who need it most. Are you ready? Let's go!

Now, if you're anything like me, you might be wondering, "But where do I even begin to find these pro bono opportunities?" Well, fear not, for I have some tips to guide you on your noble quest.

First up, let's talk about your local non-profit organizations. Many of these fine establishments are on the lookout for talented legal professionals like yourself to provide much-needed guidance and support to the Spanish-speaking communities they serve. So, roll up your sleeves and get ready to make a lasting impact!

Next, consider checking out the ever-handy internet for online platforms and databases that list pro bono opportunities specifically geared towards Spanish-speaking clients. With just a few clicks, you'll be well on your way to finding the perfect pro bono project that aligns with your interests and expertise.

Don't forget to tap into that marvelous network of yours! Reach out to your fellow legal professionals, especially those who work in the public interest or with Spanish-speaking clients, and ask if they know of any pro bono opportunities in need of your unique set of skills. You never know where a friendly inquiry might lead!

And finally, why not explore the possibility of creating your own pro bono project? If you've identified a gap in legal services for Spanish-speaking communities, gather some like-minded colleagues and put your heads together to develop a solution. Not only will you be making a difference, but you'll also be blazing a trail for future generations of do-gooder legal professionals.

conclusion

the ongoing journey to master legal spanish

Brace yourselves, dear aspiring legal Spanish gurus, for we have reached the pièce de résistance of our linguistic adventure! That's right; it's time to discuss the ongoing journey to master legal Spanish. Spoiler alert: it's a never-ending quest, but that's what makes it so thrilling!

So, you've made it this far, and you might be feeling pretty confident in your newfound legal Spanish prowess. But before you start patting yourself on the back, remember that language mastery is a lifelong pursuit, especially when it comes to the ever-evolving world of law. Fear not, though, for I have some sage advice to keep you on the path to success.

First and foremost, don't ever stop learning. In the legal world, change is the only constant. So, keep your ear to the ground for new terminology, developments, and shifts in the landscape. Embrace the fact that you'll always be a student in this realm – it's what keeps life interesting!

Next, make a habit of engaging with Spanish-language legal content. Subscribe to law journals, watch courtroom dramas, or listen to podcasts. Surround yourself with the language, and it will become second nature. Plus, who doesn't love a good courtroom drama, am I right?

Then, find your tribe. Connect with other legal professionals who share your passion for the Spanish language. Together, you can swap stories, learn from one another's experiences, and navigate the wild world of legal Spanish as a team.

Also, don't forget to practice, practice, practice! Whether it's drafting legal documents, attending Spanish-language legal events, or engaging in conversation with native speakers, the more you put your skills to use, the more proficient you'll become. So, get out there and flex those linguistic muscles of yours!

Lastly, embrace the bumps in the road. Let's face it; nobody's perfect, and we all stumble from time to time. When you inevitably encounter challenges on your journey, treat them as learning opportunities rather than setbacks. It's all part of the glorious process.

the benefits of bilingualism in the legal profession

You've stuck with me this far, and it's time we discuss the pièce de résistance – the numerous benefits of bilingualism in the legal profession. That's right; becoming a bilingual legal eagle isn't just about impressing your friends at dinner parties (though that's a nice perk, too). There's a whole world of advantages out there, just waiting for you to seize!

First up, let's talk about the ever-important topic of employability. In today's globalized world, being fluent in another language is like having a golden ticket to the Chocolate Factory of legal opportunities. Employers are chomping at the bit to snag lawyers who can navigate multiple languages with ease. So, brush up on that Spanish, and watch those job offers roll in.

Then there's the sheer joy of being able to connect with a more diverse range of clients. Gone are the days when language barriers would send you into a tailspin of panic. With your newfound bilingual prowess, you'll be able to effortlessly communicate with Spanish-speaking clients, providing them with top-notch legal counsel and earning their trust and loyalty in the process.

Let's not forget the fun of learning about different legal systems. Bilingualism opens the door to understanding the nuances and intricacies of various legal systems around the world. You'll be able to appreciate the subtle differences and similarities between jurisdictions, making you a more well-rounded and knowledgeable legal professional. Knowledge is power, as they say!

And how about the brain-boosting benefits of bilingualism? That's right – learning another language is like taking your brain to the gym for a mental workout. Studies have shown that bilingualism can improve cognitive function, enhance memory, and even stave off age-related cognitive decline. So, by mastering legal Spanish, you'll be flexing those brain muscles and staying sharp as a tack!

Finally, there's the sheer satisfaction of overcoming a challenge. Learning a new language, especially one as complex as legal Spanish, is no easy feat. But as you conquer this linguistic mountain, you'll reap the rewards of personal growth, increased confidence, and the knowledge that you can tackle anything life throws your way.

encouragement and motivation for continued language learning

As we embark on this final stretch of our linguistic adventure, I feel it's my duty to provide you with a hearty dose of encouragement and motivation for your ongoing language-learning journey. After all, Rome wasn't built in a day, and neither was your legal Spanish prowess. But fear not, for I am here to remind you of the fantastic rewards that await you!

First and foremost, it's essential to recognize that language learning is a marathon, not a sprint. Take a moment to give yourself a pat on the back for every vocabulary word learned, every grammar rule conquered, and every conversation navigated. Every little triumph is a stepping stone on your path to fluency, and you deserve to celebrate each one!

Remember that progress is not always linear. There will be days when you feel like you've hit a wall and can't possibly learn another subjunctive conjugation. But hang in there, intrepid linguist! Embrace the ups and downs, knowing that setbacks are merely opportunities for growth and self-improvement. You'll come out the other side stronger and more resilient, I promise.

Next up, let's talk about the power of community. Surround yourself with like-minded language learners and native speakers, whether that's in a class, at a meetup, or even online. Sharing your experiences, triumphs, and challenges with others on a similar journey can provide the motivation you need to keep going, even when the going gets tough.

Keep your eyes on the prize, and remind yourself of your "why." Why did you choose to learn legal Spanish? Was it to expand your career opportunities? Connect with a wider range of clients? Or simply to challenge yourself and grow personally? Whatever your reason, use it as your North Star to guide you through the inevitable rough patches and keep you focused on your ultimate goal.

Lastly, don't forget to have fun with it! Learning a new language is a wondrous, enriching experience that can open your mind to new ideas, cultures, and perspectives. So, embrace the journey with enthusiasm, humor, and a healthy dose of curiosity. After all, life is too short to take ourselves too seriously.

appendices

common spanish verbs and their conjugations

Ah, verb conjugation, the proverbial bread and butter of language learning! There's nothing quite like the feeling of accomplishment when you've finally nailed those pesky conjugations, am I right? So, without further ado, let's dive into the wacky and wonderful world of common Spanish verbs and their conjugations.

First, let's talk about the big three: ser (to be), estar (to be), and tener (to have). Yes, you read that correctly—Spanish has not one, but two verbs for "to be." But don't worry, we'll tackle them together, one conjugation at a time.

Ser is all about essence and identity. Think of

things that are permanent or intrinsic to a person or thing. Here's how you conjugate ser in the present tense:

- Yo soy (I am)
- Tú eres (you are, informal)
- Él/ella/usted es (he/she/you formal are)
- Nosotros/nosotras somos (we are)
- Vosotros/vosotras sois (you all are, informal)
- Ellos/ellas/ustedes son (they/you all formal are)

Estar, on the other hand, deals with temporary states and locations. Here's the present tense conjugation for estar:

- Yo estoy (I am)
- Tú estás (you are, informal)
- Él/ella/usted está (he/she/you formal are)
- Nosotros/nosotras estamos (we are)
- Vosotros/vosotras estáis (you all are, informal)
- Ellos/ellas/ustedes están (they/you all formal are)

Now, let's move on to tener, which is all about possession. Here's the present tense conjugation for tener:

- Yo tengo (I have)
- Tú tienes (you have, informal)
- Él/ella/usted tiene (he/she/you formal have)
- Nosotros/nosotras tenemos (we have)
- Vosotros/vosotras tenéis (you all have, informal)
- Ellos/ellas/ustedes tienen (they/you all formal have)

Once you've got these foundational verbs down, you'll be well on your way to navigating the vast ocean of Spanish conjugations. Of course, there are countless other verbs to explore, each with its own unique conjugation patterns and irregularities. But fear not, intrepid linguist! With patience, persistence, and perhaps a dash of humor, you'll master the art of Spanish conjugation in no time.

Now go forth and conjugate with gusto! And remember, practice makes perfect—or as they say in Spanish, "la práctica hace al maestro." Happy conjugating!

spanish-english legal glossary

Oh, legal jargon! What better way to impress your friends, family, and colleagues than by casually tossing around terms like "tort" and "habeas corpus"? Get ready, because we're about to embark on a whirlwind tour of some essential Spanish-English legal terms that will make you sound like a linguistic virtuoso in no time.

1. Abogado/a (ah-boh-GAH-doh/dah) - Lawyer
2. Acuerdo (ah-KWEHR-doh) - Agreement
3. Acta (AHK-tah) - Record
4. Acusación (ah-koo-sah-see-OHN) - Accusation
5. Apelación (ah-peh-lah-see-OHN) - Appeal
6. Arrendamiento (ah-rrehn-dah-MYEN-toh) - Lease
7. Asesor/a (ah-seh-SOHR/rah) - Advisor
8. Audiencia (ow-dee-EHN-see-ah) - Hearing
9. Bancarrota (bahn-kah-ROH-tah) - Bankruptcy
10. Beneficiario/a (beh-neh-fee-see-AH-ree-oh/ah) - Beneficiary
11. Caso (KAH-soh) - Case
12. Código (KOH-dee-goh) - Code

13. Compensación (kohm-pehn-sah-see-OHN) - Compensation
14. Condena (kohn-DEH-nah) - Conviction
15. Contrato (kohn-TRAH-toh) - Contract
16. Corte (KOHR-teh) - Court
17. Culpable (kool-PAH-bleh) - Guilty
18. Daño (DAH-nyoh) - Damage
19. Declaración (deh-kla-rah-see-OHN) - Declaration
20. Demanda (deh-MAHN-dah) - Lawsuit
21. Derecho (deh-REH-choh) - Right
22. Despacho (dehs-PAH-choh) - Office
23. Divorcio (dee-VOHR-see-oh) - Divorce
24. Documento (doh-koo-MEHN-toh) - Document
25. Embargo (ehm-BAHR-goh) - Seizure
26. Evidencia (eh-vee-DEHN-see-ah) - Evidence
27. Fianza (fee-AHN-sah) - Bail
28. Fraude (FRAH-oo-deh) - Fraud
29. Herencia (eh-REHN-see-ah) - Inheritance
30. Hipoteca (ee-POH-teh-kah) - Mortgage
31. Impuesto (eem-PWEHS-toh) - Tax
32. Infracción (een-frahk-see-OHN) - Infraction
33. Inquilino/a (een-kee-LEE-noh/ah) - Tenant
34. Juicio (HWEE-see-oh) - Trial

35. Juez/a (HWAYSS/ah) - Judge
36. Jurado/a (hoo-RAH-doh/dah) - Juror
37. Ley (lay) - Law
38. Licencia (lee-SEHN-see-ah) - License
39. Litigio (lee-TEE-hee-oh) - Litigation
40. Mediación (meh-dee-ah-see-OHN) - Mediation
41. Multa (MOOL-tah) - Fine
42. Notario/a (noh-TAH-ree-oh/ah) - Notary
43. Obligación (oh-blee-gah-see-OHN) - Obligation
44. Ofensa (oh-FEHN-sah) - Offense
45. Patente (pah-TEHN-teh) - Patent
46. Penal (peh-NAHL) - Penal
47. Pérdida (PEHR-dee-dah) - Loss
48. Peritaje (peh-ree-TAH-heh) - Expertise
49. Poder (poh-DEHR) - Power of attorney
50. Prisión (pree-SYOHN) - Prison
51. Prueba (PRWEH-bah) - Proof
52. Quiebra (KYEH-brah) - Bankruptcy
53. Recurso (reh-KOOR-soh) - Resource
54. Registro (reh-HEES-troh) - Registry
55. Reivindicación (ray-veen-dee-kah-see-OHN) - Claim
56. Resolución (reh-soh-loo-see-OHN) - Resolution

57. Responsabilidad (reh-spohn-sah-bee-lee-DAHD) - Liability

58. Sentencia (sen-TEHN-see-ah) - Sentence

59. Sociedad (soh-see-e-DAHD) - Partnership

60. Subasta (soo-BAHS-tah) - Auction

61. Testamento (tes-tah-MEHN-toh) - Will

62. Testigo (teh-STEE-goh) - Witness

63. Tutela (too-TEH-lah) - Guardianship

64. Víctima (VEEK-tee-mah) - Victim

65. Viuda/o (vee-OO-dah/doh) - Widow/er

66. Delito (deh-LEE-toh) - Crime

67. Demanda civil (deh-MAHN-dah thee-BEEL) - Civil lawsuit

68. Desalojo (deh-sah-LOH-hoh) - Eviction

69. Estado (ehs-TAH-doh) - Estate

70. Expropiación (eks-proh-pee-ah-see-OHN) - Expropriation

71. Firma (FEER-mah) - Signature

72. Incumplimiento (een-koom-plee-MYEN-toh) - Breach

73. Indemnización (een-dehm-nee-see-ah-see-OHN) - Compensation

74. Intereses (een-teh-REH-sehs) - Interest

75. Legítima defensa (leh-HEE-tee-mah deh-FEHN-sah) - Self-defense

76. Manutención (mah-noo-ten-see-OHN) - Maintenance

77. Nulidad (noo-lee-DAHD) - Nullity
78. Pensión (pen-see-OHN) - Pension
79. Propiedad intelectual (proh-pee-e-DAHD een-teh-lek-choo-AHL) - Intellectual property
80. Querella (keh-REH-yah) - Complaint
81. Reclamación (reh-klah-mah-see-OHN) - Claim
82. Recurso de amparo (reh-KOOR-soh deh AHN-pah-roh) - Constitutional complaint
83. Renuncia (reh-NOON-see-ah) - Resignation
84. Reparación (reh-pah-rah-see-OHN) - Reparation
85. Robo (ROH-boh) - Theft
86. Secuestro (seh-KWEHS-troh) - Kidnapping
87. Sociedad anónima (soh-see-e-DAHD ah-NOH-nee-mah) - Corporation
88. Sucesión (soo-seh-see-OHN) - Succession
89. Testaferro (tes-tah-FEH-roh) - Front man
90. Tráfico (TRAH-fee-koh) - Trafficking
91. Tribunal (tree-boo-NAHL) - Tribunal
92. Usurpación (oo-soor-pah-see-OHN) - Usurpation
93. Violación (bee-oh-lah-see-OHN) - Violation
94. Arreglo extrajudicial (ah-REH-gloh eks-trah-hoo-dee-see-AL) - Out-of-court

settlement

95. Constitución (kohn-stee-too-see-OHN) - Constitution

96. Costas procesales (KOH-stahs proh-seh-SAH-lehs) - Legal costs

97. Incomparecencia (een-kom-pah-reh-see-EN-syah) - Failure to appear

98. Jurisprudencia (hoo-rees-proo-DEHN-see-ah) - Jurisprudence

99. Prevaricación (preh-vah-ree-kah-see-OHN) - Breach of public duty

100. Presunción de inocencia (preh-soon-see-OHN deh ee-noh-THEN-see-ah) - Presumption of innocence

Now that you've got a taste of some key Spanish-English legal terms, don't be shy about sprinkling them into your daily conversations, whether you're discussing your latest case or just ordering a cup of coffee. You never know when you might need to drop some legal knowledge on an unsuspecting interlocutor!

But remember, this is just the tip of the iceberg when it comes to legal terminology. There's a whole world of Spanish-English legal terms out there, ripe for the picking. So, grab your favorite legal dictionary, cozy up in your favorite reading nook, and prepare to expand your linguistic horizons. Happy glossary-ing!

sample bilingual legal documents

Step right up, legal language enthusiasts! Today, we present to you a smorgasbord of delectable, bilingual legal documents that will tickle your linguistic taste buds. So, pull up a chair, grab your reading glasses, and prepare to feast your eyes on these tantalizing texts. Bon appétit!

Sample #1: Power of Attorney (Poder Notarial)

Ah, the classic Power of Attorney – a versatile dish that can be easily customized to suit your client's preferences. Our bilingual recipe includes both English and Spanish, ensuring that your client can fully understand their rights and responsibilities, no matter which language they prefer.

Sample #2: Lease Agreement (Contrato de Arrendamiento)

Featuring a delightful blend of terms and conditions, this Lease Agreement sample is the pièce de résistance of any landlord-tenant relationship. This bilingual beauty ensures that both parties understand their obligations, and with a dash of humor, you can make it a true masterpiece.

Sample #3: Last Will and Testament (Testamento)

Ah, the Last Will and Testament – a bittersweet concoction of bequests, legacies, and final wishes. This bilingual version is the perfect dish to serve your clients, ensuring their last hurrah is well understood by all parties involved.

Sample #4: Divorce Agreement (Convenio de Divorcio)

Though it may be a bitter pill to swallow, our bilingual Divorce Agreement sample is a must-have for navigating the choppy waters of separation. Designed to make the process more palatable, this legal document is a lifesaver in difficult times.

Sample #5: Non-Disclosure Agreement (Acuerdo de Confidencialidad)

Every good chef knows that some recipes are meant to be kept secret. That's where our Non-Disclosure Agreement comes in! This bilingual version is perfect for ensuring that everyone understands the importance of keeping your trade secrets under wraps.

These sample documents are just the beginning, my friends. As you continue on your journey to bilingual legal mastery, you'll discover a veritable buffet of legal documents waiting to be savored. So, sharpen your pencils, dust off your keyboards, and get ready to create some mouthwatering masterpieces of your own.

additional resources for further study

And now, dear readers, the moment you've been waiting for – the pièce de résistance, the cherry on top, the grand finale: a delightful collection of additional resources to satisfy your insatiable appetite for legal Spanish knowledge! Think of it as a treasure trove of linguistic goodies, just waiting to be explored.

Resource #1: Legal Spanish Books

Who doesn't love curling up with a good book? Expand your library with these page-turners that will elevate your legal Spanish game to new heights. From textbooks to dictionaries, there's a little something for everyone in this literary lineup.

Resource #2: Online Courses and Webinars

Craving a more interactive learning experience? Fear not! The internet is chock-full of courses and webinars that cater to every palate – from the novice legal Spanish learner to the seasoned bilingual attorney. With a click of a button, you can gain access to a wealth of knowledge from experts around the globe.

Resource #3: Podcasts and YouTube Channels

For the busy bees among us, podcasts and YouTube channels offer a perfect on-the-go learning experience. Tune in during your daily commute, while working out, or even while doing household chores. It's a win-win: you can flex those brain muscles and multitask like a boss!

Resource #4: Language Learning Apps

In this digital age, language learning apps are a must-have for every aspiring bilingual legal professional. From vocabulary builders to grammar quizzes, these pocket-sized tools are a fun and effective way to sharpen your legal Spanish skills during those spare moments of the day.

Resource #5: Professional Associations and Networking Groups

Last but not least, don't forget to tap into the power of professional associations and networking groups. By connecting with fellow legal Spanish enthusiasts, you can share resources, exchange ideas, and forge valuable relationships that will enrich your linguistic journey.

There you have it, folks – a tantalizing smorgasbord of resources to fuel your legal Spanish adventure! With these tools at your disposal, the sky's the limit. So, buckle up, and get ready to embark on a thrilling ride through the world of bilingual legal mastery. Happy learning!

9 798215 408735